Published in the United States of America by
Abingdon Press, 201 Eighth Avenue South, Nashville, Tennessee 37202
ISBN 0-687-49709-4

First edition 2006

Editorial Director Annette Reynolds
Editor Nicola Bull
Art Director Gerald Rogers
Pre-production Krystyna Kowalska Hewitt
Production John Laister

Printed and bound in Singapore

JENNY

STEPHANIE JEFFS
AND JACQUI THOMAS

Jenny's sister, Rosie, was not well. She didn't have a sore throat, and she didn't have a runny nose. She didn't have spots and she didn't feel sick. But Rosie was still unwell.

6

Jenny and Rosie went to the same school. Before Rosie was ill they had played in the playground together. Rosie could run fast. She could run much faster than Jenny.

9

Now Rosie had to stay at home. Jenny drew Rosie a picture to cheer her up. Rosie's teacher, Mr Philips, sent her a note and a book.

"Get well soon!" he wrote.

Rosie could speak like Mr Philips. It made Jenny laugh.

"Get well soon, Rosie!" she would say, in his funny voice.

11

Most of the time Rosie stayed in bed.

When she wasn't sleeping, Jenny would bring in her toys and play with them on the bed.

Rosie's knees were the mountains. Jenny's helicopter circled above them, while Rosie's tractor ploughed the fields. They lined up the ducks along the pillow. The cows and the sheep got lost in the quilt.

Once Rosie tucked a little lamb under her pillow. Jenny could just see his head peeping out.

"The lamb isn't very well," said Rosie. "He's hurt."

"I don't want the lamb to be hurt," said Jenny, trying to grab it.

"It'll be all right," said Rosie firmly. "The farmer will take care of it."

14

Sometimes, Rosie had to go into the hospital.

Jenny liked the drinks machine which had hot chocolate. Rosie liked it too, but when she felt ill she didn't feel like drinking chocolate.

"I hope Rosie gets well soon," said Jenny as she skipped down the hall. "Then she can have hot chocolate too!"

15

Rosie's friends made her a big card. They drew lots of kisses on it, and wrote their names inside.

Sometimes Rosie had lots of presents, and sometimes she had lots of visitors.

When Granny came, she read Rosie a story. When Ruth came, she told Rosie jokes. When Grandad came, he held Rosie's hand and stroked her cheek.

"Lord Jesus," he said, with his eyes closed, "please take care of Rosie."

Everyone who came to visit said, "Get well soon!"

They all said, "I do hope Rosie gets better soon!"

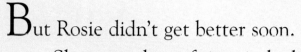But Rosie didn't get better soon.

    She spent lots of time in bed and she never played outside.

    She didn't want to plough the fields any more. She was far too tired. She hurt too much.

One day Jenny went to a farm with some friends. Rosie stayed at home in bed.

Chloe and Alice fed the ducks, while Jenny and Jack fed the baby lambs. They played on the tractor, and ran round and round until they were dizzy.

"Now what are your names?" asked the farmer. He had a funny voice. He held a tiny lamb in the crook of his arm, and gently stroked its head as he spoke.

"Alice is my sister, and Jack's my brother," said Chloe. "Jenny's my friend."

"My sister is called Rosie," said Jenny. "But she couldn't come, because she's not very well."

"Oh dear," said the farmer. "Like this little lamb here." He held out the lamb for Jenny to stroke. "I hope Rosie gets better soon."

When Jenny got into the car to go home, she felt very tired.

"Are you feeling all right?" asked Chloe's mom, as they drove home.

Jenny shook her head. She wanted to go home. She missed Rosie. She wanted to tell her about the farm and the ducks and sheep. She wanted to tell her what the farmer had said, and how he had said it. Then Rosie would speak with his funny voice and Jenny would laugh. She wanted to tell her about the little lamb, and how the farmer had held it in his arms.

But when she got home, Mom said that Rosie was asleep.

Jenny began to cry. She didn't feel ill. She just felt sad.

Jenny sat down with Mom. Mom felt her forehead.

"I expect you'll feel better after a good night's sleep," said Mom, giving her a kiss.

Jenny nodded. She knew that she would.

"Mom," said Jenny suddenly. "Why doesn't Rosie feel better after a good night's sleep? Why does everyone say that they hope she gets better soon, but she never does? Why is she always ill?"

25

Mom didn't speak for quite a while.

"Rosie may not get better," said Mom.

Jenny looked at Mom. "Never?" she asked.

"I don't think so," said Mom. There were tears in her eyes.

"That's not fair!" said Jenny, hugging her knees. "I want Rosie to get better!"

"I know it's not fair," said Mom. "I want Rosie to get better too. Everyone does. Daddy does, Granny does, Grandad does, the doctors do…"

"Is Rosie going to die?" Jenny asked.

Mom held Jenny very tight. "Yes, I think she might," she said quietly. "We must be very brave for Rosie's sake."

Jenny looked up at Mom. "Will Jesus take care of Rosie, like Grandad asked?" she said.

"Of course he will," said Mom. "He promises to take care of all of us, even when we die. He makes a special place for us to live with him in heaven. It's a place where we will never hurt again and we will always be better."

When Jenny went upstairs, she crept into Rosie's room. Rosie was fast asleep.

Quietly and carefully, Jenny lined up the ducks along the pillow. She took the sheep and the cows and dotted them around the quilt. She put the tractor in the field.

Then Jenny thought about the farmer and the little lamb who wasn't well. She wished that Rosie would wake up and never hurt again. She wished Rosie would run and laugh.

She thought how happy they had
been together.

Jenny felt very sad. Very
gently, she tucked the little
lamb under Rosie's
pillow.

"Good night,
Rosie," whispered
Jenny. Her tears
made a wet patch
on the quilt.

"Lord Jesus, please
take care of Rosie," she
said in her smallest
voice. And deep inside
she knew that he had
heard her prayer.

E
Jeffs, Stephanie.
Jenny :[coming to terms
 with the death of a si